**Based on the novelization
by Ted Conner**

**Based on the screenplay by
Dan Harris, Mike Dougherty
and David Hayter**

LEVEL 2

Adapted by: Paul Shipton

Commissioning Editor: Helen Parker

Editor: Helen Parker

Designer: Susen Vural

Cover layout: Emily Spencer

Picture research: Emma Bree

Photo credits: Cover image and film stills provided
courtesy of Marvel Characters, Inc. [other credits to follow]

CONTENTS PAGE

THE X-MEN

The X-Men are a team of mutants.
Mutants are people with special powers.

PROFESSOR X

He is also called
Charles Xavier. He has
a school for mutants.
He can read minds and
also use his power over
people's minds.

CYCLOPS

The strong beam
from his eyes
can break through
anything.

JEAN GREY

She can move things
with her mind and
read other people's
minds.

BOBBY DRAKE

He is also called Iceman
because he can make
and use ice.

ROGUE

She can take the power
of other mutants for a
short time.

STORM

She has power over
the weather. Her eyes
go white when she uses
her power.

4

THE HUMAN

WILLIAM STRYKER

This scientist hates all mutants.

LOGAN

He is sometimes called Wolverine. He is very strong. Metal claws come out of his hands and he has metal through his body.

THE OTHER MUTANTS

MAGNETO

He is also called Eric Lensherr. He can move metal things with his mind.

MYSTIQUE

This blue mutant can change her face and body to look like anyone.

NIGHTCRAWLER

He is also called Kurt Wagner. He is blue. He can disappear and appear again in a different place.

PYRO

He is also called John Allerdyce. He has power over fire.

JASON STRYKER

He is William Stryker's son. He can make people see and hear anything.

PLACES

Washington, DC: The President of the USA lives here, in the White House.
Westchester, New York: Professor X's school for mutants is here.
Boston: This is a big city and area east of New York.
Lake Alkali: This is in Canada. There is a dam across Lake Alkali.

CHAPTER 1 THE MUTANT AT THE WHITE HOUSE

The White House, Washington, DC. President McKenna was working at his desk. All around the building, guards were looking for anything unusual.

A strange man in a hat and dark glasses walked up to one guard.

'Excuse me, are you lost?' asked the guard.

The man didn't answer. Suddenly the man jumped up over the guard and started to run really fast. Everything happened very quickly. Guards took out their guns, people shouted into radios: 'We have a problem. Move President McKenna!'

A guard fired his gun, but – BAMF! – the strange man disappeared in a cloud of dark blue smoke. BAMF! He appeared again, closer to the guard, and hit him. His hat and glasses were off now. The man was dark blue – a mutant*!

Doors and walls couldn't stop this mutant. BAMF! BAMF! BAMF! He continued to disappear and appear again in a different place. Then he hit another guard and disappeared again. He was very fast and he was jumping everywhere. Nobody could hit him.

* A mutant is someone with special powers.

President McKenna was behind a wall of guards, all with their guns out and ready. It was no good. BAMF! BAMF! More guards fell and then the mutant had McKenna against his desk. He took out a knife, held it high, and then …

One of McKenna's men fired his gun and hit the mutant in the arm. BAMF! The mutant dropped the knife and disappeared again. This time he didn't come back.

President Mckenna looked at the knife next to him in the desk. It had a sign on it with just three words: FREE MUTANTS NOW!

There were mountains all around the cold waters of Lake Alkali in Canada. There were trees and snow for miles around, but no people, nobody except Logan.

He was here because he wanted to discover his past. What happened to him here years ago? Who put metal in his body and metal claws in his hands? He remembered nothing. Charles Xavier – Professor X – sent him here. Maybe here he could find some answers.

There were buildings, but they were all empty. His past was still as empty as the land around him.

Storm was one of Professor X's mutant team called the X-Men. She was also a teacher at his school for young mutants. Today, the students were at a museum and Storm was telling the younger children about humans from the past.

Jean Grey was also one of the X-Men and a teacher at the school. She was at the museum, too. But today there was a problem. Suddenly she could hear everything people were thinking. That was part of Jean's power – to read the minds of others. But her power wasn't usually this strong, and it was impossible to stop.

'Jean, are you OK?' asked her boyfriend, Cyclops. He was also one of the X-Men.

'I … I'm fine,' she answered.

But Cyclops knew her very well. 'You've been different these last few weeks,' he said.

'You know I can read people's minds,' answered Jean with a frightened look. 'But now I can hear *everything*.'

'And that's not all, is it?' Cyclops asked.

It was true. Jean's other power – to move things with her mind – was also much stronger now.

'My dreams are getting worse,' she said. 'I think something terrible is going to happen …'

Cyclops held her in his arms. 'Nothing is going to happen to you. I will not let it.'

Three teenagers from the school – Rogue, Bobby and John – sat in the museum café. John was playing with a lighter in his hand – *on, off, on, off.*

Two human teenagers stood next to him. 'It's an easy question,' said one of the teenagers. 'Can I have a light?'

'Why are you being so stupid?' asked the other teenager.

John just smiled. 'Because I can.'

'Can I have a light?' The teenager's voice was angry now. *On, off, on, off.* 'Sorry, I can't help you,' laughed John.

'Stop this, John,' said Bobby. He didn't want any trouble.

'I'm just having some fun,' said John, but then one of the human teenagers pulled the lighter from his hand. He gave John an unfriendly smile. It was a big mistake. John, also called Pyro, was a mutant with power over fire. Suddenly the teenager's arm was on fire. He fell back and cried out. John just laughed.

Bobby was on his feet. He used *his* power – over ice – and the fire went out.

The human teenager gave them a frightened look. First fire, then ice. What was happening? All around them people were looking.

Then suddenly everybody stopped, everything was

quiet. Nobody in the museum moved, except the mutants.

John looked around in surprise. 'Did *you* do this?' he asked Bobby.

'No,' said a deep voice. 'I did.'

It was Charles Xavier – Professor X. He had power over other people's minds and he was using this now on all the humans in the museum. He was looking at John. 'If you want to use your power outside again, *don't*,' he said angrily.

The only other sound came from a TV at the back of the café. The mutants turned to it. There was a news story. It was about the mutant at the White House.

'It's time to leave,' said Cyclops.

'You're right,' answered Xavier.

A moment later, the humans in the museum were moving and talking again.

The X-Men were back at the school in Westchester. They were discussing the mutant at the White House.

'I think this is Magneto's work,' said Cyclops.

'I don't agree,' said Jean.

Professor X wasn't sure. But they all knew one thing – this was a big problem for every mutant. Now humans were going to hate mutants even more. Mutants were going to be in even more danger. They *had* to find the mutant from the White House.

'I have tried to find him with Cerebro,' said Xavier. The machine, Cerebro, helped Xavier to find people and to read their minds. 'But he's moving all the time. I'm going to try again. And then, Jean and Storm, you will go and get him.'

A scientist called William Stryker was in President McKenna's office.

'What is it, William?' asked McKenna.

'I want to do some special work on the mutant problem.'

Another man came into the room.

'This is Senator Robert Kelly,' said McKenna. 'He's worked on the mutant question for a long time.'

Stryker looked at Kelly. 'But haven't your ideas about mutants changed?' asked the scientist.

Kelly smiled. 'Yes, I understand them a lot better now, I think.'

Stryker began to explain his plan. He put down a photo of a building – Professor X's school. 'Mutants are training here,' he said, 'not far from the city of New York.'

'Where did you get this information?' asked McKenna.

'From a mutant we have in prison,' said Stryker. 'He's called Eric Lensherr.'

Kelly looked up. 'Ah, you have Magneto?'

'Yes,' said Stryker. 'We built his special prison. Magneto can't use his power there.'

McKenna looked at the photo. 'OK, William,' he said. 'You can send in some soldiers and look around. But be careful. I don't want any dead children on the TV news.'

Outside the office, Kelly spoke to Stryker. 'I would like to see Magneto,' he said.

'That won't be possible,' Stryker answered.

'Do you really want to start a fight between humans and mutants?' asked Kelly.

'It has always been a fight,' said Stryker, 'and *we* are going to win.'

As Stryker left, Kelly's eyes turned yellow. This wasn't really Senator Kelly – he was dead. This was a mutant called Mystique. She had the power to look like anybody. And now she had information about her friend, Magneto …

CHAPTER 2 NIGHTCRAWLER

Rogue liked life at Professor X's school, and she *really* liked Bobby Drake. Bobby liked her, too, but there was a problem. When he tried to kiss her, Rogue moved her head away.

'I … don't want to hurt you,' she said.

'I'm not frightened,' smiled Bobby. But Rogue knew it was very dangerous. When she touched people, she took their power. She could even kill people with her touch.

Rogue heard a sound outside the room. Logan was back! She ran out and Bobby followed.

'Are you happy to see me?' Logan asked.

'Not really,' answered Rogue, but her eyes and smile told the true story.

Logan looked at Bobby. 'Who's this?'

'This is Bobby. He's …'

'I'm her boyfriend,' said Bobby. 'Call me Iceman.'

Then, there was a voice from the stairs. 'Hi, Logan.'

'Hi, Jean,' he answered.

Jean Grey had a boyfriend, Cyclops. Logan knew this, but he still loved her. And maybe, just maybe, she liked him, too.

'Storm and I are leaving soon in the X-Jet*,' she said. 'We're going to find the mutant from the White House.' She smiled. 'Will you be here when we come back?'

Logan looked into Jean's eyes. 'I'll be here.'

Then Cyclops came down the stairs. He wasn't happy to see Logan.

'You were looking for something,' he said. 'Did you find it?'

Logan's eyes were still on Jean. 'Yes, I think so.'

Magneto's prison was very special. There was no metal anywhere so Magneto couldn't use his power to escape.

The doors opened and William Stryker walked in with a big guard.

'It's very kind of you to visit,' said Magneto.

But Stryker wasn't listening. The guard hit Magneto across the head and pushed his face down onto the table. Stryker injected something into the back of Magneto's neck. Then Magneto just sat there very still. His eyes were empty now. He was ready to follow Stryker's orders.

'Tell me more about Professor X's school,' said the scientist, 'and the machine called Cerebro.'

* The X-Jet is the X-Men's super fast plane.

Professor X was sitting at Cerebro when Logan found him. Xavier put on the special helmet. 'Don't move,' he told Logan.

Suddenly there were white lights all around the big room.

'These lights are all the humans in the world,' said Xavier.

Then the colour of the lights changed to red. Now there weren't as many.

'The red lights are the mutants. Cerebro allows me to 'see' their minds. It joins me to them.' Professor X looked at just one light. 'I'm trying to find the mutant from the White House, but it isn't easy.'

'Can't you just think harder?' asked Logan.

'Yes, if I want to kill him.'

But suddenly Professor X said, 'There! He isn't running now. I can see him!'

Xavier turned off the machine. He wanted to tell the other X-Men about the mutant.

'Wait!' said Logan. 'I want you to read my mind again. I have to know my past.'

Professor X looked at Logan. 'It won't help. Sometimes the mind needs to discover things for itself.' He moved to the door. 'Logan, can you stay here with the students tonight? Cyclops and I are going to see an old friend.'

Mystique was still in Washington, DC. She didn't look like Senator Kelly any more. Now she looked like Yuriko Oyama, one of Stryker's helpers. As Yuriko, it was easy for her to go into the building where Stryker worked. She found his office and sat down at his computer.

'Stryker, William,' she said in Stryker's voice. The computer let her in and she read about Magneto and his prison. Then she looked carefully at the faces of all the guards at the prison. She chose one and remembered his name.

Before she left, Mystique saw another name on the computer – Cerebro. What could Stryker know about that? Quickly she found a computer picture of Professor X's machine. Mystique didn't understand, but there was no time to think. There was a sound behind her. Yuriko Oyama – the *real* Yuriko – was coming.

Quickly, Mystique changed. Now she looked like the office cleaner.

'What are you doing here?' asked the *real* Yuriko.

But the 'cleaner' didn't speak English. He said something in Spanish then left the office.

Storm and Jean Grey went into the quiet, dark church in Boston. The mutant from the White House was *somewhere* in here. But where?

Suddenly a voice shouted out in German. There was a strange sound. BAMF! Then there were shouts from high up in the church.

Jean looked at Storm. 'He's a Teleporter. He can disappear and appear again in a different place,' she said.

'We just want to talk,' shouted Storm to the mutant. But he didn't come down.

Storm's eyes went white as she used her special power over the weather. Suddenly there was a strong wind right there, inside the church. The dark blue mutant started to fall, but he didn't hit the floor. Jean stopped him with the power of her mind.

'You're not going anywhere now,' said Jean. 'Are you?'

'Please don't kill me!' cried the mutant.

The mutant was German and his name was Kurt Wagner. He also used the name Nightcrawler. He told Storm and Jean about the White House. 'There were guns everywhere. I was very frightened. I could see it all, but I couldn't stop myself. It was like a bad dream …'

'Did anything happen to you before you went to the White House?' asked Storm.

'Nothing. I was here.'

'We need to take him to Professor X,' said Jean.

Then Jean saw something on the back of Nightcrawler's neck. 'What's that?' she asked. It was round and looked exactly like the back of Magneto's neck where Stryker injected him.

CHAPTER 3 ESCAPE FROM THE SCHOOL

Logan was dreaming about his past …

He was on his back … there were doctors and scientists around him … 'You will remember nothing of your old life,' … Then he felt hot metal, as hot as fire … Everything was dark and then he was running, running into the light …

Logan woke up in the dark. He tried to remember his dreams, but he couldn't. And he couldn't go back to sleep now.

The school was quiet, but Logan wasn't the only one not asleep. Bobby was in the kitchen.

'Does *anybody* sleep around here?' asked Logan. He got a drink from the cupboard and gave the bottle to Bobby. The teenager touched it and the drink was cold.

'Thanks,' said Logan.

'No problem.'

'So how long have you been here?'

'Two years,' said Bobby. 'My parents don't know I'm a mutant. They think this is an ordinary school.'

'So what about you and Rogue?'

'We … like each other,' Bobby said slowly. 'But it's not easy when you can't be close to someone.

Logan understood. He wanted to be close to someone, too, but it wasn't possible.

Professor X and Cyclops went to visit Magneto in his prison. Professor X went into Magneto's room and Cyclops waited at the entrance.

'Have you come to save me, Charles?' asked Magneto.

'Not today, Eric,' Xavier answered. 'I want to talk to you about the mutant at the White House. What do you know?'

'Nothing.' Magneto turned and Xavier saw the lines on his white face. He looked old and very, very tired.

'What has happened to you?' Xavier asked in surprise.

'I've had some visits from William Stryker,' said Magneto. 'You remember him. His son, Jason, was one of your students.'

'Yes, years ago,' said Xavier. 'I wasn't able to help him.'

'And now you've let Logan into your school,' smiled Magneto. 'Have you told him about his past with Stryker?'

Magneto looked different and he was talking in a strange way. Something was very wrong.

'Eric, what have you done?' asked Xavier.

'I ... I couldn't stop myself.'

'What have you told Stryker?' asked Professor X.

It was hard for Magneto to answer. 'Everything,' he said.

Professor X turned – he had to get back to his school!

But it was too late. The doors didn't open. Stryker had Magneto in his prison, and now he had Professor X.

Outside the room, Yuriko Oyama had a gun in her hand. She fired it at Cyclops. The X-Man hit her with the special beam from his eyes and she fell against the wall. Very quickly she got back up and jumped at Cyclops. She jumped much faster and higher than any human – Yuriko was a mutant, too! She hit Cyclops in the head, and he fell to the floor.

Logan was still in the kitchen when he heard a sound outside the room. He went to look … and saw a soldier with a gun! Logan moved fast and held the soldier from behind by the arms.

'You chose the wrong place,' said Logan.

The soldier fought back and started to fire his gun. But suddenly – SNIKT! – Logan's claws came out and he pushed them into the soldier.

There were lots of other soldiers in the school. Some of them fired at the students with special guns, and the young mutants fell to the floor, asleep. Other students used their powers to escape. One girl ran right through the walls.

There were frightened children everywhere. Shouts. Lights in the dark, and more and more soldiers. Logan's claws stayed out. He hit one soldier, then another and another. He was like a killing machine.

A tall student called Colossus took some of the children into a secret tunnel. In another part of the school, Bobby was looking for Rogue. He found her and he also found John – Pyro.

The three teenagers ran towards a window. No good.

There were soldiers there, too. They ran back the other way, into a big room. There, lights shone in their faces – *more* soldiers. What could they do? But then they heard a shout from above and Logan jumped down to the floor. His metal claws shone in the dark. There was blood everywhere as Logan killed the soldiers one by one.

More soldiers were coming.

'Let's go!' Logan shouted.

They ran to the secret tunnel, but Logan didn't follow the three teenagers. He turned back, claws out. He was ready to fight or die.

'Try and kill me!' he shouted at the soldiers.

'No, don't!' shouted a voice from the dark. 'Not yet.'

Logan knew that voice from somewhere.

'Is that you, Wolverine?' the man continued. 'What a

surprise! How long has it been? Fifteen years? You haven't changed a bit.'

The man walked into the light. It was William Stryker.

The three teenagers ran through the tunnel.

'Wait!' shouted Rogue. 'We can't leave Logan. They'll kill him!'

Pyro didn't want to go back, so Rogue looked at her boyfriend.

'Bobby, please!' she said.

Logan was looking at Stryker. 'Who are you?' he said.

'Don't you remember?' the man smiled. 'I'm William Stryker.'

Logan started to move towards him. He needed to know about his past. Maybe this man had the answers.

But suddenly there was something in front of Logan – a wall of ice. Only one person could do that. Bobby and the other teenagers were back to help him.

'Come on, Logan,' called Rogue from the tunnel entrance. 'Let's go!' He looked back at them. 'Go! I'll be fine!'

'But *we* won't,' she said.

Logan understood – at that moment it was more

important to help these young mutants. He ran to the
tunnel. Moments later, Stryker and his soldiers crashed
through the wall of ice. But there was no one on the other
side.

Logan and the teenagers ran through the tunnel. They
reached a garage and found Cyclops' car. Moments later,
they were driving very quickly through the dark.

'Who *was* that man?' asked Pyro.

'His name's Stryker,' said Logan.

'Who is he?'

'I … can't remember.' Logan drove even faster. 'Storm
and Jean are in Boston. We'll go there.'

'My parents live in Boston,' said Bobby.

William Stryker walked through the school. He couldn't
find Logan, but that was OK. He wasn't really there to
find mutants. He wanted something else – he wanted
Cerebro.

CHAPTER 4 MUTANT 143

The TV news was about the mutant problem, but Mitchell Laurio wasn't listening. After a long day as a guard at Magneto's prison, he just wanted a drink.

A beautiful woman was sitting at the bar. 'Do you want another drink?' she asked and pushed a glass towards him. 'My name's Grace.'

This wasn't true, but Laurio didn't know that.

There was something in the bottom of his drink, but he didn't know that either.

The woman's real name was Mystique! And minutes later, when the guard was asleep, she injected something into him.

Professor X was in a dark room at Stryker's base. There was a small machine on his head. 'That machine keeps you out of *here*,' said Stryker and he touched his own head.

'Where's Cyclops?' asked Professor X.

'Don't worry,' answered Stryker. 'I'm teaching him some *new* ideas. You know all about that, don't you?' He was talking about his own son's time at Professor X's school.

'You wanted me to make Jason *better*,' said Professor X. 'But I couldn't do that. Mutants aren't *ill*.'

'You're lying!' shouted Stryker. 'You were frightened of him! After he left your school, he used his power at home on us. In the end, my wife killed herself.'

There was a sound from the back of the room. It was Stryker's helper, Yuriko. She was looking all around her. She looked suddenly surprised to be there. Quickly, Stryker walked over to her and injected something into the back of her neck. After that, she was quiet again. And then Xavier understood. Stryker was injecting mutants so they followed his orders.

'*You* sent that mutant to the White House,' Xavier said. 'You wanted people to hate mutants even more.'

'Yes, you're right,' answered Stryker. 'I've worked with mutants for a long time, but I've never found the answers to the most important questions. How many mutants are there in the world? How can we find them? Nobody really knows – except you.' He looked right at Professor X. 'I can't inject you because your mind is too strong. But there is another way …'

The door opened and Yuriko brought someone into the room. The man wore hospital clothes and a machine went from his chair into the back of his neck. His eyes were empty and he looked almost dead.

'Meet Mutant 143,' said Stryker.

Professor X couldn't believe it. 'This is Jason, your son,' he said. 'What have you done to him?'

'My son is dead,' said Stryker. 'Just like all mutants.'

He left the room, and now Professor X was alone with Jason.

'Hello! Is anybody home?' called Bobby.

There was no answer – Bobby's family home was empty.

Rogue was still wearing her night clothes, so Bobby took her upstairs to get some different clothes. Downstairs Pyro looked at all the photos of Bobby's family. The happy faces didn't look much like *his* family.

Rogue had new clothes on now, but she and Bobby didn't go downstairs yet. Bobby moved closer to her. He saw the frightened look in her eyes. 'I'll be OK,' he said.

And then they kissed. At first it was fantastic, but then Bobby felt it – something was pulling the life out of his body.

She moved away quickly. 'I'm sorry,' she said.

Bobby's parents and younger brother came home.

'Who are *you*?' shouted Bobby's father when he saw Logan.

Bobby was already running down the stairs. 'This is Professor Logan,' he said. 'He's … a teacher at my school.' He looked at his parents. 'I have to tell you something .'

Mitchell Laurio brought Magneto his meal. Magneto stood up and smiled. 'Something is different about you today, Mr Laurio.'

'Sit down!' ordered Laurio.

'No.' Magneto lifted his hand and suddenly the guard couldn't move.

'What are you doing?' cried the guard.

There was metal somewhere in the room – it was inside Laurio's body. Mystique injected it into him the night before.

Magneto moved his hand and little bits of

metal flew out of Laurio's body in a cloud. The guard fell to the floor. He was dead.

Magneto moved his hand again and the bits of metal came together into three balls. These flew at the prison walls and broke them into a thousand pieces.

Nothing could stop Magneto now. It was time to leave this place.

It was uncomfortably quiet at the Drake family home. Now his parents knew about their son's power.

'We still love you, Bobby,' his mother said. 'It's just this mutant problem …'

'What *problem*?' asked Logan angrily.

'Just see Bobby's power,' Rogue said.

Bobby touched his mother's cup of hot coffee. A moment later, it was ice.

'And I can do a lot more than that,' said Bobby.

But his brother didn't want to hear any more. He jumped up and ran to his bedroom. Moments later he was on the phone. 'Please send the police.'

Logan was in the garden when he heard the radio in Cyclops' car. It was Jean and Storm from the X-Jet. They were flying back to the school with Nightcrawler. When they got no answer from the school in Westchester, they tried Cyclops' car radio. Logan told them quickly about Stryker's soldiers at the school.

'We're on our way to get you,' said Jean.

But, as Logan went back to the house, he saw something at the front of the house – police!

He ran to the house and shouted to the teenagers,

'We have to go!'

But they were too late. There were police officers everywhere with guns out.

Suddenly – SNIKT! – Logan's claws came out. 'Drop the knives and put your hands up!' shouted an officer.

'I can't,' said Logan. The claws were a part of him. 'Look!'

He moved his hand to show the claws, but the police officer was frightened. BANG! He fired the gun. It hit Logan in the head and the mutant fell. Was he dead?

The police ordered the three teenagers to lie down. But Pyro didn't lie down. His lighter was in his hand. 'You know all those dangerous mutants on the news?' he said. 'I'm the worst!'

Suddenly, there was a ball of fire in his hands. He threw

the fire at one police officer, then another. After that, he turned to the police cars. BOOM! The fire hit one car, then another and another. There was fire and smoke everywhere, and Pyro was enjoying it. He *loved* to use his power.

Someone had to stop him. Rogue reached out and touched Pyro's leg. After a few moments, he looked terrible. His power and his life were leaving him, going into Rogue. She held up her hand and all the fires went out.

Logan opened his eyes. He wasn't dead! His body had the power to make itself better even after something terrible like that.

Suddenly, there was a loud noise above them. The X-Jet was coming down. Storm and Jean were here! The mutants ran towards the plane. Bobby turned and looked at his home and his family in the window. And then he followed the others to the plane.

CHAPTER 5 LAKE ALKALI

Professor X was standing at a window in the school. He was looking out at the gardens. He turned and smiled …

Wait! Something was wrong! Professor X wasn't able to stand. He lost the use of his legs long ago.

'Jason, stop it!' cried Xavier. He looked around. He wasn't in the school, he was still in the base with Jason Stryker. Jason had a very special power over other people's minds. He played tricks with them. He could make them see and hear things. But these things weren't really there. Jason put them into people's minds. His power was very strong and even Professor X couldn't fight it. It was happening again …

He was back in the school again. Everything was quiet except for the sound of a young girl. She was crying.

'You can come out now,' said Xavier.

When she came out, he asked, 'Where are all the other children?'

'I don't know.'

Xavier smiled. 'Let's find them. We'll use Cerebro …'

The X-Men were near the school when suddenly a fighter plane appeared in the sky. 'Follow us to our base. That's an order!' said a voice on the radio.

But it was impossible – they had to find Professor X and the others. Jean used her mind power to escape from the fighter. And Storm used her weather power. At last they lost the plane in the dark storm clouds. But then …

'Oh no, here's another one!' cried Storm.

A second fighter plane was right behind them.
Suddenly two missiles were flying towards the X-Jet.
There wasn't time for Storm to do anything. But Jean
could. Her power was stronger than ever. With her mind
she moved the first missile away from them. But the
second missile was still coming. Jean moved it a little, but
it was too late. The missile hit the X-Jet! Then the plane
was falling and falling. They couldn't do anything to stop
it. They were going to die.

But the X-Jet didn't crash. It slowed and then stopped.
Everyone was safe.

'Is that you, Jean?' shouted Storm.

'No, it's not me!'

The X-Men looked down from the plane and saw the
answer. It was Magneto.

The mutants sat around a fire and Magneto explained about Stryker.

'He came to your school because he wanted Cerebro. He wants to build a copy of it.'

'But only Professor X can use Cerebro,' said Jean.

'Stryker has got the Professor,' continued Magneto. 'With Xavier's power he can use Cerebro to kill every mutant in the world.'

The X-Men were quiet.

'Why do you need us?' asked Storm.

'Mystique has discovered information about a secret base. Stryker is building the second Cerebro there. But where's the base? Do you know?'

Jean didn't know, but somebody here did. Stryker used Nightcrawler at the White House. The answer must be with the dark blue mutant.

Moments later, the others watched as Jean put her hands on Nightcrawler's head. She started to read his mind …

He was in a dark room. Someone injected him in the neck. Outside there was snow and water, lots of cold water …

Jean pulled her hands away. 'Stryker's base is at Lake Alkali in Canada.'

'But I went to Lake Alkali,' said Logan. 'There's nothing there.'

'The base isn't up on the top,' said Jean. 'You have to go down to reach it.'

Logan was thinking about Stryker when Jean found him later that night.

'Are you OK?' she asked.

'Are *you*?' he said.

'I'm worried about Cyclops. I love him.'

Logan's eyes met hers. 'Do you?' He knew one thing about himself – he was in love with Jean.

Jean liked Logan, too. She couldn't hide it, and so Logan kissed her.

'Please,' she said. 'Don't make me do this.'

'Do what?'

'This.'

And she walked away.

The next day the mutants flew in the X-Jet to Lake Alkali. Magneto was sitting with Mystique.

'What's your name?' Magneto asked the teenager with the lighter.

'John Allerdyce.'

'What's your *real* name?'

John showed a small ball of fire in his hand. 'Pyro,' he answered.

'Never forget this, Pyro,' said Magneto. 'Next to you, humans are *nothing*.'

'The new Cerebro is ready,' said one of Stryker's men.

'Good,' answered the scientist. He was looking at six

young mutants from Professor X's school on a TV.

'Why are we keeping the children here?' asked the soldier.

'I'm a scientist,' said Stryker. 'When I build a machine, I want to test it.'

The X-Jet arrived at Lake Alkali.

'This is a map of the area,' Storm explained. 'The dam holds back all the water. This tunnel is the entrance to Stryker's base. But we can't just go in. Stryker will fill the tunnel with water. Someone has to go in first and reach the dam's main computer.'

'Can you get in?' Storm asked Nightcrawler.

'Not when I don't know a place. It's too dangerous,' he answered.

'I'll go,' said Logan quietly. 'Stryker won't kill *me*.'

'No,' said Magneto. 'I have a better plan.'

He looked at Mystique and she smiled.

'There's someone in the tunnel,' said one of Stryker's men.

Stryker looked up at the TV. Logan was there and he was looking right at the camera.

'Wolverine's coming home,' smiled Stryker. 'Bring him to me.'

CHAPTER 6 THE NEW CEREBRO

Stryker took one look at Logan. 'I know my own work,' he said. 'This isn't Logan. Kill this mutant, then close the doors!'

The soldiers pulled out their guns, but the mutant changed. It was Mystique! Two big metal doors were closing. Mystique jumped through them before anyone could hit her.

She found the computer room and started to work very quickly. Soon the tunnel doors were open and the other X-Men could come in.

Professor X was back in the school. He was sitting at Cerebro. 'You can come in,' he told the little girl. She followed him inside the machine.

In the real world, Jason Stryker followed Professor X into the new Cerebro.

The doors of the computer room opened. It was Magneto and the X-Men!

'Have you found Cerebro?' Magneto asked Mystique.

She touched a map on the computer. 'Here.'

'We must go there now,' said Magneto.

'I'm coming, too,' Jean told him.

Storm was looking at a TV in the room. It showed six mutant children from the school.

'We have to get them,' Storm said. 'Will you help me, Nightcrawler?'

Logan was watching another TV. This one showed Stryker in another part of the base. He ran to the door. He needed to speak to Stryker about his past.

Stryker was at the new Cerebro. He spoke quietly into Jason's ear.

'It's time to find our friends,' he said.

The little girl came closer to Xavier.

'It's time to find our friends,' she said.

'It's time to find all the mutants,' Stryker told his son.

'It's time to find all the mutants,' the little girl said to Professor X.

Xavier put the Cerebro helmet on his head and Stryker left the room. Moments later, there were red lights everywhere. The new Cerebro was working. It was joining Professor X's mind to all the mutants in the world.

Magneto, Mystique and Jean were on their way to Cerebro. Suddenly Jean stopped. Something was wrong. A tall man came around the corner. It was Cyclops. He fired his beam at them from his eyes. He was under Stryker's power!

Jean pushed Magneto and Mystique away just in time.

'Go!' she shouted. 'I'll stop him!'

She pushed Cyclops as hard as possible with her mind. He flew back and hit the wall. But then he got up and fired another beam from his eyes. It almost hit Jean. Her mind stopped it like a wall in front of her.

'Cyclops, don't do this!' she shouted.

She pushed with her mind even harder.

Cyclops fell back and the beam from his eyes went everywhere. It crashed through machines, walls, and anything in its way. It broke through part of the dam. The water of Lake Alkali started to come through the wall.

Jean looked up. Cyclops was walking towards her.

'Jean, it's OK. It's me,' he said. 'I'm so sorry. I could see you, but I couldn't stop myself.'

He took her in his arms and kissed her. 'I love you, Jean.'

Logan was in another part of the base – a dark room with machines everywhere. He knew this place and he started to remember …

He escaped from here years ago … As he ran through a tunnel towards the light, he saw his claws for the first time …

'The hot metal over there is called adamantium,' said a voice behind him. 'When it's cold, it is the strongest metal in the world. Nothing can break it.'

It was Stryker, and Yuriko was with him.

'At one time there was nobody like you, Logan,' continued Stryker. 'Not any more …'

Stryker left the room, but Yuriko stayed. Suddenly – SNIKT! – long metal claws appeared from her hands.

The two mutants began to fight, but Yuriko was faster than Logan. Her claws shone in the light as she hit Logan again and again. Logan fell back and Yuriko jumped at him. Quickly, he moved his hands and pushed his claws into her body.

But Yuriko didn't die. She was like Logan in another way, too. Her body could make itself better after almost anything.

The fight continued. Yuriko hit him with her claws again and again. She was going to kill him. Was this the end for Logan?

He reached for the machine with the hot metal. He pushed it into Yuriko's body and turned the machine on. The metal disappeared into her.

Their eyes met for a moment. Then metal came out of Yuriko's eyes and mouth. Seconds later she was dead.

'Find all the mutants,' the little girl told Professor X. 'Find them all. Now kill them!'

All around the base, the mutants cried out – Storm, Mystique, Jean and Cyclops, the mutant children … They all fell to the floor. They didn't know it, but the new Cerebro was killing them.

Only Magneto was safe because he was wearing a special helmet. He stood outside Cerebro and used his power to pull metal pieces from the machine. The machine stopped working. Now all the mutants were safe.

Magneto opened the metal doors and walked into the room. He smiled at Jason coldly. Professor X was still under Jason's power, but Magneto did nothing to help him. Instead, he used his power to put Cerebro together again. Then Mystique changed to look like William

Stryker. She used Stryker's voice to speak into Jason's ear. 'The plan has changed. Find all the humans!'

Magneto put a hand on Xavier's arm. 'Goodbye, Charles,' he told his old friend.

Then he and Mystique left.

'The plan has changed,' said the little girl to Professor X. 'Find all the humans!'

CHAPTER 7 A BETTER FUTURE?

Stryker was outside the base. He had to escape. He had to get to his plane. Logan followed him. He hit the scientist, then pushed him hard against the side of the plane.

'You took my life!' Logan shouted. 'Why did you put that metal in my body? Why did you give me claws?'

'I'm a scientist and you were my work,' said Stryker. 'You wanted it!'

'Who am I?'

'Do you really want to know about your past?' Stryker tried to smile. 'Then come with me now.'

There was a loud sound from far away.

'What's that?' asked Logan.

'The dam. Something has broken it. In a few minutes, this area will be under water. Your friends will die. Come with me and I'll tell you everything.'

But Logan picked up a long thin piece of metal and put it around Stryker and one of the plane wheels. 'Now you can't move,' he said. 'If we die, you die.'

Then Logan ran back to the base. He had to help the other X-Men. He had to help Jean.

Storm and Nightcrawler found the six children from the school. The children were safe now. Then they went to the doors of Cerebro. At that moment Jean and Cyclops came around the corner.

'What's happening inside?' asked Storm.

Jean used her power to find out. 'Professor X is still in there,' she said. 'He's with another mutant. He's in a dream of some kind. Oh no! Magneto has changed

Cerebro. Now Professor X is going to kill everyone *except* the mutants! All the humans in the world are going to die!'

What could the X-Men do? It was too dangerous for Cyclops to break the door open with the beam from his eyes.

Storm looked at Nightcrawler. 'I need you to take me inside.'

He knew it was very dangerous, but there was no other way.

'Don't believe anything in there,' Jean told them. And then … BAMF! Nightcrawler and Storm disappeared in a cloud of dark blue smoke.

'Hello,' said the little girl. 'Who are you looking for?'

Storm and Nightcrawler were inside Cerebro, but they couldn't see Professor X.

'Professor, can you hear me?' shouted Storm. 'Stop Cerebro now!'

'Who are you talking to?' asked the girl.

Nightcrawler moved towards the girl, but Storm held him back. 'Don't move!'

'But she's just a little girl.'

Storm knew better. 'No, she's not,' she said.

Magneto and Mystique were outside the base now. They found Stryker at his plane.

'Mr Stryker,' said Magneto coldly. 'We meet again – for the last time!'

They got into the plane with Pyro and flew away.

Storm turned to Nightcrawler. 'It's going to get very cold in here,' she said.

'I'm not going anywhere,' answered the dark blue mutant.

Storm's eyes went white and she started to use her power.

'What are you doing?' asked the little girl.

Storm said nothing. The room was becoming colder and colder.

'Stop it!' shouted the little girl. 'My father is going to be so angry with me!'

'Jason!' It was Professor X's voice.

Jason couldn't use his power in this terrible cold. Xavier pulled the Cerebro helmet from his head and turned around.

The little girl wasn't there any more. Professor X saw just the real world – Jason, Storm and Nightcrawler.

But there was still a problem. Very soon the dam was going to break completely. The walls of Cerebro were falling. They had to leave this place fast. Quickly, Nightcrawler took Storm outside – BAMF! And then Professor X – BAMF!

But sadly there was no time to save Mutant 143, Jason Stryker.

More water was coming into the base. Soon everything was going to be under water.

The X-Men ran with the children. Storm and Nightcrawler carried Professor X.

They were almost at the tunnel when the metal doors closed. Logan was standing by the doors.

'You don't want to go that way,' he said. 'The water's coming. There's another way out!'

The rest of the team followed him outside.

'Stryker's plane was right here!' shouted Logan. 'It's gone!'

Suddenly another plane appeared over the trees. It was the X-Jet, and Rogue was flying it. She was just a teenager and she was very frightened. The plane went to one side, then the other, but at last she brought it down.

Only Logan didn't go to the plane. He could hear something. Or was it someone? Logan went through the trees. Stryker was on a wall now. He was dying.

'Who has the answers, Logan?' he said. 'Mutants?'

Logan turned. 'I think maybe they do.'

Stryker shouted after him. 'One day someone will finish my work, Wolverine!'

But Logan didn't look back as he ran to the X-Jet.

The X-Men weren't safe yet. 'The computer isn't working,' said Cyclops.

Cyclops and Storm tried to start the plane.

'Oh no! We've lost the power!' said Storm.

And then the dam broke. The water was coming towards them. Inside the plane, only Jean knew this. And only she could do anything about it.

She took a last look at the X-Men, at Logan and her boyfriend, Cyclops. And then she left the plane.

'Where's Jean?' asked Cyclops a few moments later.

'She's outside,' said Professor X.

'No!' Cyclops ran for the door, but Jean used her power to close it.

The power of Jean Grey's mind was never stronger. She made a wall against the waters from the dam. At the same time she lifted the plane up and turned on its power. In her last moments she sent her thoughts to Professor X. He spoke Jean's words for her: 'This is the only way … Goodbye!'

The plane was above the water and ready to fly. The X-Men were safe.

Jean Grey closed her eyes and disappeared under the waters of Lake Alkali.

President McKenna was going to speak to his people about the country's biggest problem – mutants. He sat in front of the TV camera.

A man said, 'We're live in five, four, three, two …'

McKenna started: 'This is a difficult time for the United States. There is a problem in this country and it is growing. We have to do something …'

Suddenly, the camera went off. The room became dark. Everybody except President McKenna stopped. Nobody moved or spoke. It was Professor X and his X-Men.

'Good morning, Mr President,' said Xavier. 'Please don't be frightened.'

'Who are you?'

'We're mutants.'

Rogue put some papers on McKenna's desk. 'These are from the office of William Stryker,' said Xavier.

McKenna read them quickly. They showed Stryker's plan against all mutants.

McKenna sat down. 'I've never seen this information before.'

'Some people think humans and mutants can never be friends,' said Professor X. 'Your words were true. This *is* a difficult time. It is a time to decide. Will we fight, or will we work together for a better future?'

Back at the school in Westchester, Professor X was talking to Logan and Cyclops.

'Why?' asked Logan. 'Why did Jean leave the plane?'

'She made a choice,' said Xavier.

A group of students came to the door, and the two X-Men left.

'Listen,' Logan said to Cyclops. 'She did make a choice. It was you.'

Cyclops walked away sadly.

Back in the office, Xavier looked at his class. Nothing could bring Jean back, but the future was here, in the young faces of his students.

'Is everything OK, Professor?' asked one girl.

Charles Xavier looked out through the window. 'Yes. I think it will be.'

THE FILM

People loved the first X-Men film, and director Bryan Singer and his team now had a difficult job. They wanted to make the second X-Men film even better. They did it! It opened in May 2003 in 3,741 cinemas in the USA – more than any other film before that time.

The director Bryan Singer with Patrick Stewart (Professor X)

WRITING THE FILM

The director worked with the writers on the story for the film. They knew one thing from the start – this time the bad guys were going to be humans, not mutants.

They were already filming when Bryan Singer decided on the ending with Jean Grey. This was like a story about Jean in the X-Men comics, and it continues in the third X-Men film.

MAKING THE FILM

X-Men 2 has over 800 special effects. The film-makers made a lot of these on computers, but not all of them:

● President McKenna's office is a copy of the office in the real White House. The copy of the President's desk took two months to make.

● When Bobby Drake makes a wall of ice between Stryker and Logan, the ice is real.

● There was no snow when they were filming outside in Canada. They had to make snow!

THE X-MEN COMIC

The X-Men was a comic long before it was a film. The film makers included some special things for fans of the comic:

● When Mystique looks at Stryker's computer, a lot of the names on the screen are from the X-Men comics.

● In one scene there is part of a TV news show. A man called Hank McCoy is talking about 'the mutant problem'. Hank McCoy was one of the first team of X-Men in the comics – and he appears in the third film.

Storm in the X-Men comic

NOT IN THE FILM...

The director wanted to include some scenes in 'The Danger Room' in the film. In this secret room in Professor X's school, the X-Men practise their special powers. But in the end, they didn't have enough money to film these scenes.

They filmed some scenes but cut them out later. In one scene, Professor X and Cyclops escape from Stryker's base and fly back to the school in Westchester. When they are there, we learn that this is just another of Jason Stryker's tricks. They didn't really escape at all.

The film changes some things from the X-Men comic:

● In the comic, William Styker kills his wife and son when he learns the boy is a mutant.

● Yuriko Oyama isn't a mutant in the X-Men comics. She is half-human, half-machine, but she does have long claws like Logan.

● In the comic, Mystique is Nightcrawler's mother!

Have you seen any of the X-Men films? Which one did you like best? Why?

What do these words mean?
You can use a dictionary.
director   special   effect   fan
screen   scene   cut

THE SCIENCE OF THE X-MEN

Charles Darwin started the idea of evolution in 1859. Many people were against his ideas.

The X-Men films are interesting and exciting. But could they really happen?

EVOLUTION

In the film mutants like the X-Men are the next step in human evolution. Suddenly, evolution takes a very big jump and makes super humans with very special powers. In the real world human evolution has happened very, very slowly. It has taken millions of years for small changes to happen.

Big changes like the powers of the X-Men aren't really possible. But perhaps science will make them possible in the future?

MAGNETISM

In the film Magneto has power over anything metal. He can lift heavy metal things up into the sky. He can even use magnetism to lift himself and 'fly'.

In the real world we can use magnets to move metal things. There is a special train called the Maglev. Magnets lift the train up and it rides on the air. It is the fastest train in the world.

Of course, no living thing has Magneto's power over metal. But perhaps some birds are able to follow magnetic lines when they fly a long way.

A Maglev train in China

THE POWER OF THE MIND

In the film both Professor X and Jean Grey can read other people's minds. Many people think it is possible to read people's minds. Some scientists have done a lot of work on this power. In some experiments people have to guess pictures like these.

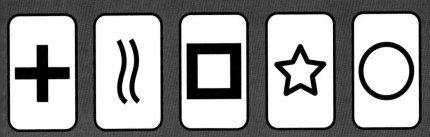

Jean Grey can also move things with her mind – she even lifts the X-Jet! Scientists have done experiments to find out about this power, too. Most scientists don't believe people can read minds or move things with their minds. But …

A man called Uri Geller became famous. He could read minds and bend metal things with the power of his mind.

A man called Derren Brown also read minds. Once he asked someone to go into another room and draw a number of simple pictures. Derren then guessed the pictures. He was right every time!

An American called David Blaine often does amazing things. He can stay under water for a week. He can live without food for more than a month.

David Blaine

Do you think humans can have special powers? In the future will science give people special powers?

Some people believe in the powers of people like Geller, Brown and Blaine. But for others, they are just clever tricks.

What do these words mean? You can use a dictionary.

science   evolution   magnet / magnetic / magnetism   experiment   amazing

THE WHITE HOUSE

At the beginning of the film, Nightcrawler goes to the White House. There, he tries to kill President McKenna. It's a very exciting moment. The White House is of course a very famous and important building. It is the home and workplace of the President of the United States of America. But what else do you know about it?

WHERE IS THE WHITE HOUSE?

The address of the White House is: 1600 Pennsylvania Avenue, Washington, DC, USA.

WHO DESIGNED THE WHITE HOUSE?

There was a competition to design a home for the President. Nine people entered the competition. An Irish man called James Hoban won. The building started on 10th November 1792 and finished on 1st November 1800. John Adams was the first President to live and work there.

WAS IT ALWAYS CALLED THE WHITE HOUSE?

At first the building was called the Executive Mansion. But people soon started to call it the White House because of the colour of the building. Theodore Roosevelt was the first President to use the name.

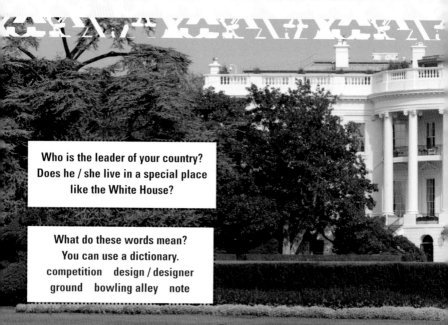

Who is the leader of your country? Does he / she live in a special place like the White House?

What do these words mean? You can use a dictionary.
competition   design / designer
ground   bowling alley   note

HOW BIG IS THE WHITE HOUSE?

In photos the White House looks quite small, but it is really very big. A lot of the building is below ground. It has 6 floors and is 5100 m².

WHERE DOES THE PRESIDENT WORK?

The President works in the west part of the house in the West Wing. The President's office is called the Oval Office.

The President's desk in the Oval Office

FUN FACTS

● The White House has 132 rooms, 35 bathrooms, 412 doors and 147 windows!

● It also has a bowling alley, a swimming pool and a cinema

● There is a picture of the White House on the back of the $20 note.

CHAPTERS 1–2

Before you read

You can use a dictionary for this section.

1 Use these words to answer the questions.

   soldier   helmet   scientist   ice   prison   neck   guard

   Which …

   a) goes on your head?

   b) is a part of the body?

   c) is very cold?

   d) is hard to escape from?

   e) fights for his / her country?

   f) discovers new ideas?

   g) looks after a place?

2 Use these words to complete the sentences.

   metal   human   claws   power   machine
   injected   mind   kissed

   a) Computers are a kind of … .

   b) … things are usually strong.

   c) All people are …

   d) Each mutant has a special … .

   e) He … his girlfriend on the mouth.

   f) The doctor … something into my arm.

   g) You use your … to think.

   h) Cats have … on their feet.

After you read

3 Answer the questions.

   a) What happens at the White House?

   b) What does Logan find at Lake Alkali?

   c) Why does Magneto follow Stryker's orders?

   d) Who discovers information about Magneto's prison?

4 What do you think?

   a) Why did Nightcrawler try to kill President McKenna?

   b) What is Mystique going to do with the information
          about Magneto?

CHAPTERS 3–4

Before you read

5 Which is which? You can use a dictionary.

base   tunnel   beam

a) Soldiers live here.

b) It's long and dark.

c) It's long and light.

6 Guess the answers to these questions.

a) Who is Professor X going to visit?

b) What will happen when William Stryker visits the school?

c) Who sent Nightcrawler to the White House? Why?

d) Can Magneto escape from prison? How?

Now read chapters 3–4. Were your guesses right?

After you read

7 Put these events in order.

a) Magneto escapes from his prison.

b) Soldiers come into the school for mutants.

c) A police officer fires a gun at Logan.

d) Bobby Drake returns to his home in Boston.

e) Stryker gets Professor X and Cyclops.

f) Logan and the three teenagers escape in a car.

8 Correct the sentences.

a) William Stryker goes to the school to find Logan.

b) Magneto injects metal into one of the prison guards.

c) Jason Stryker sent Nightcrawler to the White House.

d) William Stryker's son is dead.

e) Bobby Drake's mother calls the police.

f) Logan stops Pyro when he is going to kill the police officers.

9 What do you think?

a) What happened to Logan in the past?

b) What does Stryker plan to do with Cerebro?

CHAPTERS 5–7

Before you read

10 Match the two columns. You can use a dictionary.

   a) The **dam** holds back   **i)** the plane.

   b) The soldiers fired a **missile** at   **ii)** a lot of water.

11 All of these things happen in chapters 5–7. Who …

   a) tells the X-Men about Stryker's plan?

   b) tries to kill every mutant in the world?

   c) tries to kill every human in the world?

   d) saves the rest of the team, but dies?

After you read

12 Complete the sentences with these names.

   Nightcrawler   Magneto   Logan   Jean   Jason Stryker

   a) … plays tricks on Professor X's mind.

   b) … stops the X-Jet when the missile hits it.

   c) … reads Nightcrawler's mind.

   d) … kills Yuriko in a fight.

   e) … takes Storm into Cerebro.

13 Answer the questions.

   a) Why does Magneto save the X-Men when the X-Jet is going to crash?

   b) What does Jean discover when she reads Nightcrawler's mind?

   c) Why does Cyclops try to hit the X-Men with his beam?

   d) Why does Jean leave the plane at the end?

14 What do you think?

   a) Who is your favourite person in the book? Why? Who don't you like? Why not?

   b) Were you surprised when Magneto didn't help Xavier? Why or why not?

   c) Would people really hate and fear mutants with special powers? Why or why not?